Super Easy Air Fryer Recipes

Learn How to Cook Low-Fat and Delicious Meals Easily and Quickly with Your Air Fryer

Linda Wang

© **Copyright 2021 by Linda Wang - All rights reserved.**

The content contained within this book may not be reproduced, duplicated or transmitted without direct written permission from the author or the publisher.
Under no circumstances will any blame or legal responsibility be held against the publisher, or author, for any damages, reparation, or monetary loss due to the information contained within this book. Either directly or indirectly.

Legal Notice:
This book is copyright protected. This book is only for personal use. You cannot amend, distribute, sell, use, quote or paraphrase any part, or the content within this book, without the consent of the author or publisher.

Disclaimer Notice:
Please note the information contained within this document is for educational and entertainment purposes only. All effort has been executed to present accurate, up to date, and reliable, complete information. No warranties of any kind are declared or implied. Readers acknowledge that the author is not engaging in the rendering of legal, financial, medical or professional advice. The content within this book has been derived from various sources. Please consult a licensed professional before attempting any techniques outlined in this book.
By reading this document, the reader agrees that under no circumstances is the author responsible for any losses, direct or indirect, which are incurred as a result of the use of information contained within this document, including, but not limited to, — errors, omissions, or inaccuracies.

TABLE OF CONTENTS

INTRODUCTION..1

Fennel Frittata 5

Lemony Raspberries Bowls 7

Perfect Breakfast Frittata 8

Bacon and Egg Bite Cups 10

Delicious Doughnuts 12

Cheesy Hash Brown 14

Carrot Oatmeal 16

Basil Chicken Bites 18

Chicken and Celery Stew 20

Amazing Mac and Cheese 22

Cheese and Bacon Rolls 23

Chicken Fillet with Brie and Turkey 25

Garlic Beets 26

Rosemary Cornbread 28

Cod Fillets 30

Crab Dip 32

Cajun Salmon 34

Salmon Thyme and Parsley 35

Turkey Wings Orange Sauce 37

Barbeque Chicken Wings 39

Chicken and Squash	41
Greek Chicken	43
Herby Chicken	45
Lamb with Potatoes	46
Beef with Apples and Plums	48
Garlicky Loin Roast	50
Glazed Pork Shoulder	52
Lamb Chops with Veggies	54
Spaghetti Squash Alfredo	56
Eggplant Stacks	58
Mushrooms with Peas	60
Veggie Stuffed Bell Peppers	62
Cauliflower Soup	65
Lemony Lentil Soup	67
Kale Cottage Cheese Soup	69
Broccoli Dip	71
Mozzarella and Tomato Salad	73
Sweet Pepper Poppers	75
Crispy Shrimps	77
Croissant Rolls	79
Rice Flour Crusted Tofu	81
Strawberry Cobbler Recipe	83
Grape Stew	85

Raspberry Muffins 86

Oreo Cheesecake 88

Apple Pastry Pouch 90

Stuffed Apples 92

Cinnamon Chocolate Churros 94

Monkey Bread 96

Cinnamon Sugar Roasted Chickpeas 99

NOTES 101

INTRODUCTION

An Air Fryer is a magic revolutionized kitchen appliance that helps you fry with less or even no oil at all. This kind of product applies Rapid Air technology, which offers a new way to fry with less oil. This new invention cooks food through the circulation of superheated air and generates 80% low-fat food. Although the food is fried with less oil, you don't need to worry as the food processed by the Air Fryer still has the same taste like the food fried using the deep-frying method.

This technology uses a superheated element, which radiates heat close to the food and an exhaust fan in its lid to circulate airflow. An Air Fryer ensures that the food processed is cooked completely. The exhaust fan located at the top of the cooking chamber helps the food get the same heating temperature in every part quickly, resulting in a cooked food of better and healthier quality. Besides, cooking with an Air Fryer is also suitable for those individuals which are too busy or do not have enough time. For example, an Air Fryer only needs half a spoonful of oil and takes 10 minutes to serve a medium bowl of crispy French fries.

In addition to serving healthier food, an Air Fryer also provides some other benefits to you. Since an Air Fryer helps you fry using less oil or without oil for some kind of food, it automatically reduces the fat and cholesterol content in food. Indeed, no one will refuse to enjoy fried food without worrying about the greasy and fat content. Having fried food with no guilt is one of the pleasures of life. Besides having low fat and cholesterol, you save some amount of money by consuming oil sparingly, which can be used for other needs. An Air Fryer also can reheat your food. Sometimes, when you have fried leftover and you reheat it, it will usually serve reheated greasy food with some addition of unhealthy reuse oil. Undoubtedly, the saturated fat in the fried food gets worse because of this process. An Air Fryer helps you reheat your food without being afraid of extra oils that the food may absorb. Fried bananas, fish and chips, nuggets, or even fried chicken can be reheated to become as warm and crispy as they were before by using an Air Fryer.

Some people may think that spending some amount of money to buy a fryer is wasteful. I dare to say that they are wrong because an Air Fryer is not only used to fry. It is a sophisticated multi-function appliance since it also helps you to roast chicken, make steak, grill fish, and even bake a cake. With a built-in air filter, an Air Fryer filters the air and saves your kitchen from smoke and grease.

An air Fryer is really a new innovative method of cooking. Grab it fast and welcome to a clean and healthy kitchen.

Fennel Frittata

Preparation Time: 20 minutes

Servings: 6

Ingredients:

- 1 fennel bulb; shredded
- 6 eggs; whisked
- 2 tsp. cilantro; chopped.

- 1 tsp. sweet paprika
- Cooking spray
- A pinch of salt and black pepper

Directions:

1. Take a bowl and mix all the ingredients except the cooking spray and stir well.
2. Grease a baking pan with the cooking spray, pour the frittata mix and spread well
3. Put the pan in the Air Fryer and cook at 370°F for 15 minutes. Divide between plates and serve them for breakfast.

Nutrition:

Calories: 200; Fat: 12g; Fiber: 1g; Carbs: 5g; Protein: 8g

Lemony Raspberries Bowls

Preparation Time: 17 minutes

Servings: 2

Ingredients:

- 1 cup raspberries
- 2 tbsp. butter
- 2 tbsp. lemon juice
- 1 tsp. cinnamon powder

Directions:

1. In your air fryer, mix all the ingredients, toss, cover, cook at 350°F for 12 minutes, divide into bowls and serve for breakfast

Nutrition:

Calories: 208; Fat: 6g; Fiber: 9g; Carbs: 14g; Protein: 3g

Perfect Breakfast Frittata

Preparation Time: 10 minutes

Cooking Time: 32 minutes

Serve: 2

Ingredients:

- 3 eggs
- 2 tbsp parmesan cheese, grated
- 2 tbsp sour cream
- 1/2 cup bell pepper, chopped
- 1/4 cup onion, chopped
- 1/2 tsp pepper
- 1/2 tsp salt

Directions:

1. Add eggs in a mixing bowl and whisk with remaining ingredients.
2. Spray air fryer baking dish with cooking spray.
3. Pour egg mixture into the prepared dish and place in the air fryer and cook at 350 F for 5 minutes.
4. Serve and enjoy.

Nutrition:

Calories 227, Fat 15.2 g, Carbohydrates 6 g, Sugar 2.6 g, Protein 18.2 g, Cholesterol 271 mg

Bacon and Egg Bite Cups

Preparation Time: 15 minutes

Cooking Time: 15 minutes

Servings: 4

Ingredients:

- 6 large eggs
- ½ cup red peppers, chopped
- ¼ cup fresh spinach, chopped
- ¾ cup mozzarella cheese, shredded
- 3 slices bacon, cooked and crumbled
- 2 tablespoons heavy whipping cream
- Salt and black pepper, to taste

Directions:

1. Preheat the Air fryer to 300 degree F and grease 4 silicone molds.
2. Whisk together eggs with cream, salt and black pepper in a large bowl until combined.

3. Stir in rest of the ingredients and transfer the mixture into silicone molds.
4. Place in the Air fryer and cook for about 15 minutes.
5. Dish out and serve warm.

Nutrition:

Calories: 233, Fats: 17.2g, Carbohydrates: 2.9g, Sugar: 1.6g, Proteins: 16.8g, Sodium: 472mg

Delicious Doughnuts

Preparation Time: 28 Minutes

Servings: 6

Ingredients:

- 1/2 cup sugar
- 2 ¼ cups white flour
- 1 tsp. cinnamon powder

- 2 egg yolks
- 1/3 cup caster sugar
- 4 tbsp. butter; soft
- 1 ½ tsp. baking powder
- 1/2 cup sour cream

Directions:

1. In a bowl; mix 2 tablespoon butter with simple sugar and egg yolks and whisk well
2. Add half of the sour cream and stir.
3. In another bowls; mix flour with baking powder, stir and also add to eggs mix
4. Stir well until you obtain a dough, transfer it to a floured working surface; roll it out and cut big circles with smaller ones in the middle.
5. Brush doughnuts with the rest of the butter; heat up your air fryer at 360 degrees F; place doughnuts inside and cook them for 8 minutes
6. In a bowl; mix cinnamon with caster sugar and stir. Arrange doughnuts on plates and dip them in cinnamon and sugar before serving.

Cheesy Hash Brown

Preparation Time: 30 minutes

Servings: 6

Ingredients:

- 1½ lbs. hash browns
- 6 bacon slices; chopped.
- 8 oz. cream cheese; softened
- 1 yellow onion; chopped.
- 6 eggs

- 6 spring onions; chopped.
- 1 cup cheddar cheese; shredded
- 1 cup almond milk
- A drizzle of olive oil
- Salt and black pepper to taste

Directions:

1. Heat up your air fryer with the oil at 350°F. In a bowl, mix all other ingredients except the spring onions and whisk well
2. Add this mixture to your air fryer, cover and cook for 20 minutes
3. Divide between plates, sprinkle the spring onions on top and serve.

Carrot Oatmeal

Preparation Time: 20 minutes

Servings: 4

Ingredients:

- 1/2 cup steel cut oats
- 2 cups almond milk
- 1 cup carrots; shredded

- 2 tsp. sugar
- 1 tsp. cardamom; ground
- Cooking spray

Directions:

1. Spray your air fryer with cooking spray, add all ingredients, toss and cover. Cook at 365°F for 15 minutes. Divide into bowls and serve

Basil Chicken Bites

Preparation Time: 30 minutes

Servings: 4

Ingredients:

- 1 ½ lb. chicken breasts, skinless; boneless and cubed
- ½ cup chicken stock
- ½ tsp. basil; dried
- 2 tsp. smoked paprika

- Salt and black pepper to taste.

Directions:

1. In a pan that fits the air fryer, combine all the ingredients, toss, introduce the pan in the fryer and cook at 390°F for 25 minutes
2. Divide between plates and serve for lunch with a side salad.

Nutrition:

Calories: 223; Fat: 12g; Fiber: 2g; Carbs: 5g; Protein: 13g

Chicken and Celery Stew

Preparation Time: 35 minutes

Servings: 6

Ingredients:

- 1 lb. chicken breasts, skinless; boneless and cubed
- 4 celery stalks; chopped.
- ½ cup coconut cream
- 2 red bell peppers; chopped.

- 2 tsp. garlic; minced
- 1 tbsp. butter, soft
- Salt and black pepper to taste.

Directions:

1. Grease a baking dish that fits your air fryer with the butter, add all the ingredients in the pan and toss them.
2. Introduce the dish in the fryer, cook at 360°F for 30 minutes, divide into bowls and serve

Nutrition:

Calories: 246; Fat: 12g; Fiber: 2g; Carbs: 6g; Protein: 12g

Amazing Mac and Cheese

Preparation Time: 15 minutes

Servings: 2

Ingredients:

- 1 cup cooked macaroni
- 1/2 cup warm milk
- 1 tablespoon parmesan cheese
- 1 cup grated cheddar cheese
- salt and pepper; to taste

Directions:

1. Preheat the Air Fryer to 350 - degrees Fahrenheit. Stir all of the ingredients; except Parmesan, in a baking dish.
2. Place the dish inside the Air Fryer and cook for 10 minutes. Top with the Parmesan cheese.

Cheese and Bacon Rolls

Preparation Time: 25 minutes

Servings: 3

Ingredients:

- 8 ounces. refrigerated crescent roll dough [usually 1 can]
- 6 ounces. very sharp cheddar cheese; grated
- 1-pound bacon; cooked and chopped

Directions:

1. Unroll the crescent dough and, using a sharp knife, cut it into 1-inch by 1 1/2 - inch pieces.
2. In a medium bowl; combine the cheese and bacon. Spread about 1/4 cup of this mixture on each piece of dough.
3. Briefly preheat your Air Fryer to 330 – degrees Fahrenheit.
4. Place the rolls in the Fryer; either on the Air Fry tray or in the food basket.

5. Bake until golden brown; 6 – 8 minutes, and enjoy!

6. Note: The timing of this recipe can vary from one Fryer to the next; so watch carefully for the browning of the rolls.

Chicken Fillet with Brie and Turkey

Preparation Time: 40 minutes

Servings: 2

Ingredients:

- 4 slices turkey [cured]
- 2 chicken fillets [large]
- 4 slices brie cheese
- 1 tablespoon chives [chopped]
- pepper and salt to taste

Directions:

1. Preheat Air Fryer to 360 - degrees Fahrenheit. Cut chicken fillets into 4 pieces and season with salt and pepper.
2. Add chives and brie to it.
3. Add the ingredients onto the plain piece of turkey.
4. Close and wrap Turkey. Hold closed with toothpick. Air fry for 15 minutes, then roast until brown.

Garlic Beets

Preparation Time: 10 minutes

Cooking time: 25 minutes

Servings: 4

Ingredients:

- 2 pounds beets, peeled and roughly cubed
- A pinch of salt and black pepper
- 1 teaspoon chili powder
- 4 garlic cloves, minced
- 1 tablespoon olive oil

Directions:

1. In your air fryer's basket, combine the beets with salt, pepper and the other Ingredients:, toss and cook at 370 degrees F for 25 minutes.
2. Divide the beets between plates and serve as a side dish.

Nutrition:

Calories 171, fat 4, fiber 2, carbs 13, protein 3

Rosemary Cornbread

Preparation Time: 1 hr.

Servings: 6

Ingredients:

- 1 cup cornmeal
- 1 ½ cups of flour
- 1/2 teaspoon baking soda
- 1/2 teaspoon baking powder
- 1/4 teaspoon kosher salt
- 1 teaspoon dried rosemary
- 1/4 teaspoon garlic powder
- 2 tablespoons caster sugar
- two eggs
- 1/4 cup melted butter
- 1 cup buttermilk
- 1/2 cup corn kernels

Directions:

1. In a bowl; mix all dry Ingredients until well combined. In another bowl, combine all liquid Ingredients
2. Add the liquid mix to the dry mix. Fold in the corn kernels and stir to combine well.
3. Press the batter into the round loaf pan that is lightly greased with a non-stick cooking spray. Air-fry for 1 hour at 380 - degrees Fahrenheit.

Cod Fillets

Preparation Time: 20 minutes

Servings: 4

Ingredients:

- 4 cod fillets; boneless
- 1 fennel; sliced

- 2 garlic cloves; minced
- 1 red bell pepper; chopped.
- 2 tbsp. olive oil
- 1 tbsp. thyme; chopped.
- ½ tsp. black peppercorns
- 2 tsp. Italian seasoning
- A pinch of salt and black pepper

Directions:

1. Take a bowl and mix the fennel with bell pepper and the other ingredients except the fish fillets and toss.
2. Put this into a pan that fits the air fryer, add the fish on top
3. Introduce the pan in your air fryer and cook at 380°F for 15 minutes. Divide between plates and serve.

Nutrition:

Calories: 241; Fat: 12g; Fiber: 4g; Carbs: 7g; Protein: 11g

Crab Dip

Preparation Time: 18 minutes

Servings: 4

Ingredients:

- 8 oz. full-fat cream cheese; softened.
- 2: 6-oz.cans lump crabmeat
- ¼ cup chopped pickled jalapeños.
- ¼ cup full-fat sour cream.
- ¼ cup sliced green onion
- ½ cup shredded Cheddar cheese
- ¼ cup full-fat mayonnaise
- 1 tbsp. lemon juice
- ½ tsp. hot sauce

Directions:

1. Place all ingredients into a 4-cup round baking dish and stir until fully combined. Place dish into the air fryer basket

2. Adjust the temperature to 400 Degrees F and set the timer for 8 minutes. Dip will be bubbling and hot when done. Serve warm.

Nutrition:

Calories: 441; Protein: 17.8g; Fiber: 0.6g; Fat: 33.8g; Carbs: 8.2g

Cajun Salmon

Preparation time: 10 minutes

Servings: 1-2

Ingredients:

- Salmon fillet – ¾-inch thick: 1)
- Juice of ¼ lemon
- For Breading: Cajun seasoning for coating
- Optional: Sprinkle of sugar

Directions:

1. Warm the Air Fryer to 356º Fahrenheit : approx. 5 min.).
2. Rinse and pat the salmon dry. Thoroughly coat the fish with the coating mix.
3. Arrange the fillet in the fryer basket and set the timer for seven minutes with the skin side facing upward.
4. Serve with a drizzle of lemon.

Salmon Thyme and Parsley

Preparation Time: 25 Minutes

Servings: 4

Ingredients:

- 4 salmon fillets; boneless
- 4 thyme springs
- 4 parsley springs

- 3 tbsp. extra virgin olive oil
- 1 yellow onion; chopped
- 3 tomatoes; sliced
- Juice from 1 lemon
- Salt and black pepper to the taste

Directions:

1. Drizzle 1 tablespoon oil in a pan that fits your air fryer; add a layer of tomatoes, salt and pepper, drizzle 1 more tablespoon oil, add fish, season them with salt and pepper, drizzle the rest of the oil, add thyme and parsley springs, onions, lemon juice, salt and pepper, place in your air fryer's basket
2. Cook at 360°F, for 12 minutes shaking once. Divide everything on plates and serve right away

Turkey Wings Orange Sauce

Preparation Time: 45 minutes

Servings: 4

Ingredients:

- 2 turkey wings
- 1½ cups cranberries
- 1 cup orange juice

- 2 tbsp. butter; melted
- 1 yellow onion; sliced
- 1 bunch thyme; roughly chopped.
- Salt and black pepper to taste

Directions:

1. Place the butter in a pan that fits your air fryer and heat up over medium-high heat.
2. Add the cranberries, salt, pepper, onions and orange juice; whisk and cook for 3 minutes
3. Add the turkey wings, toss and cook for 3-4 minutes more
4. Transfer the pan to your air fryer and cook at 380°F for 25 minutes
5. Add the thyme, toss and divide everything between plates. Serve and enjoy!

Barbeque Chicken Wings

Preparation Time: 40 minutes

Servings: 4

Ingredients:

- 1/2 cup BBQ sauce
- 2 lbs. chicken wings; cut into drumettes and flats

Directions:

1. Set the temperature of Air Fryer to 380°F. Grease an Air Fryer basket. Arrange chicken wings into the prepared Air Fryer basket in a single layer.
2. Air Fry for about 24 minutes, flipping once halfway through. Now, set the temperature of Air Fryer to 400°F.
3. Air Fry for about 6 minutes. Remove from Air Fryer and transfer the chicken wings into a bowl. Drizzle with the BBQ sauce and toss to coat well. Serve immediately.

Chicken and Squash

Preparation Time: 35 minutes

Servings: 4

Ingredients:

- 14 oz. coconut milk
- 6 cups squash; cubed
- 8 chicken drumsticks
- 1/2 cup cilantro; chopped.
- 2 tbsp. olive oil
- 2 tbsp. green curry paste
- 1/4 tsp. coriander; ground
- 1/2 cup basil; chopped.
- 2 red chilies; minced
- 3 garlic cloves; minced
- A pinch of cumin; ground
- Salt and black pepper to taste

Directions:

1. Heat up a pan that fits your air fryer with the oil over medium heat.
2. Add the garlic, chilies, curry paste, cumin, coriander, salt and pepper; stir and cook for 3-4 minutes.
3. Add the chicken pieces and the coconut milk and stir
4. Place the pan in the fryer and cook at 380°F for 15 minutes
5. Add the squash, cilantro and basil; toss and cook for 5-6 minutes more. Divide into bowls and serve. Enjoy!

Greek Chicken

Preparation Time: 10 minutes

Cooking Time: 24 minutes

Serve: 4

Ingredients:

- 2 lbs chicken tenders
- 1 cup cherry tomatoes
- 2 tbsp olive oil
- 3 dill sprigs
- 1 large zucchini
- For topping:
- 2 tbsp feta cheese, crumbled
- 1 tbsp fresh dill, chopped
- 1 tbsp olive oil
- 1 tbsp fresh lemon juice

Directions:

1. Preheat the air fryer to 370 F.
2. Spray air fryer basket with cooking spray.

3. Add chicken, zucchini, dill, and tomatoes into the air fryer basket. Drizzle with olive oil and season with salt.
4. Cook chicken for 24 minutes.
5. Meanwhile, in a small bowl, stir together all topping ingredients.
6. Place chicken on the serving plate then top with veggies and discard dill sprigs.
7. Sprinkle topping mixture on top of chicken and vegetables.
8. Serve and enjoy.

Nutrition:

Calories 555, Fat 28 g, Carbohydrates 5.2 g, Sugar 3 g, Protein 68 g, Cholesterol 205 mg

Herby Chicken

Cooking Time: 15 minutes

Servings: 2

Ingredients:

- 2 chicken breasts
- Mixed herb chicken seasoning
- 2 tbsp. soft cheese
- Salt and pepper; to taste

Directions:

1. Preheat air fryer at 356°F. Score the chicken by partly slicing into the breasts for the seasoning. Season with salt and pepper, then using your hands, cover the chicken in the soft cheese
2. Roll the chicken breasts in the mixed herbs and place in the air fryer on a reusable baking mat. Cook at 356°F for 15 minutes or until cooked in the middle. Serve.

Lamb with Potatoes

Preparation Time: 20 minutes

Cooking Time: 15 minutes

Servings: 2

Ingredients:

- ½ pound lamb meat
- 2 small potatoes, peeled and halved
- ½ small onion, peeled and halved
- ¼ cup frozen sweet potato fries
- 1 garlic clove, crushed
- ½ tablespoon dried rosemary, crushed
- 1 teaspoon olive oil

Directions:

1. Preheat the Air fryer to 355 degree F and arrange a divider in the Air fryer.
2. Rub the lamb evenly with garlic and rosemary and place on one side of Air fryer divider.

3. Cook for about 20 minutes and meanwhile, microwave the potatoes for about 4 minutes.
4. Dish out the potatoes in a large bowl and stir in the olive oil and onions.
5. Transfer into the Air fryer divider and change the side of lamb ramp.
6. Cook for about 15 minutes, flipping once in between and dish out in a bowl.

Nutrition:

Calories: 399, Fat: 18.5g, Carbohydrates: 32.3g, Sugar: 3.8g, Protein: 24.5g, Sodium: 104mg

Beef with Apples and Plums

Preparation time: 10 minutes

Cooking time: 30 minutes

Servings: 4

Ingredients:

- 2pounds beef stew meat, cubed
- 1cup apples, cored and cubed
- 1cup plums, pitted and halved
- 2tablespoons butter, melted

- Salt and black pepper to the taste
- ½ cup red wine
- 1tablespoon chives, chopped

Directions:

1. In the air fryer's pan, mix the beef with the apples and the other ingredients, toss, put the pan in the machine and cook at 390 degrees F for 30 minutes.
2. Divide the mix between plates and serve right away.

Nutrition:

Calories 290, Fat 12, Fiber 5, Carbs 19, Protein 28

Garlicky Loin Roast

Preparation Time: 60 minutes

Servings: 4

Ingredients:

- 1 lb. pork loin roast
- 3 garlic cloves; minced
- 2 tbsp. panko breadcrumbs
- 1 tbsp. olive oil
- 1 tbsp. rosemary; chopped.

- Salt and black pepper to taste

Directions:

1. Place all ingredients except the roast into a bowl; stir / mix well.
2. Spread the mixture over the roast. Place the roast in the air fryer and cook at 360°F for 55 minutes
3. Slice the roast, divide it between plates and serve with a side salad

Glazed Pork Shoulder

Servings: 5

Preparation Time: 15 minutes

Cooking Time: 18 minutes

Ingredients

- 1/3 cup soy sauce
- 2 tablespoons sugar
- 1 tablespoon honey
- 2 pounds pork shoulder, cut into 1½-inch thick slices

Directions:

1. In a bowl, mix together all the soy sauce, sugar, and honey.
2. Add the pork and generously coat with marinade.
3. Cover and refrigerate to marinate for about 4-6 hours.
4. Set the temperature of air fryer to 335 degrees F. Grease an air fryer basket.

5. Place pork shoulder into the prepared air fryer basket.
6. Air fry for about 10 minutes and then, another 6-8 minutes at 390 degrees F.
7. Remove from air fryer and transfer the pork shoulder onto a platter.
8. With a piece of foil, cover the pork for about 10 minutes before serving.
9. Enjoy!

Nutrition:

Calories: 475, Carbohydrate: 8g, Protein: 36.1g, Fat: 32.4g, Sugar: 7.1g, Sodium: 165mg

Lamb Chops with Veggies

Servings: 4

Preparation Time: 20 minutes

Cooking Time: 8 minutes

Ingredients

- 2 tablespoons fresh rosemary, minced
- 2 tablespoons fresh mint leaves, minced
- 1 garlic clove, minced
- 3 tablespoons olive oil
- Salt and ground black pepper, as required
- 4: 6-ounceslamb chops
- 1 purple carrot, peeled and cubed
- 1 yellow carrot, peeled and cubed
- 1 parsnip, peeled and cubed
- 1 fennel bulb, cubed

Directions:

1. In a large bowl, mix together the herbs, garlic, oil, salt, and black pepper.

2. Add the chops and generously coat with mixture.
3. Refrigerate to marinate for about 3 hours.
4. In a large pan of water, soak the vegetables for about 15 minutes.
5. Drain the vegetables completely.
6. Set the temperature of air fryer to 390 degrees F. Grease an air fryer basket.
7. Arrange chops into the prepared air fryer basket in a single layer.
8. Air Fry for about 2 minutes.
9. Remove chops from the air fryer.
10. Place vegetables into the air fryer basket and top with the chops in a single layer.
11. Air Fry for about 6 minutes.
12. Remove from air fryer and transfer the chops and vegetables onto serving plates.
13. Serve hot.

Nutrition:

Calories: 470, Carbohydrate: 14.8g, Protein: 49.4g, Fat: 23.5g, Sugar: 3.1g, Sodium: 186mg

Spaghetti Squash Alfredo.

Preparation Time: 25 minutes

Servings: 2

Ingredients:

- ½ large cooked spaghetti squash
- ¼ cup grated vegetarian Parmesan cheese.
- ½ cup shredded Italian blend cheese
- ½ cup low-carb Alfredo sauce
- 2 tbsp. salted butter; melted.
- ¼ tsp. ground peppercorn
- ½ tsp. garlic powder.
- 1 tsp. dried parsley.

Directions:

1. Using a fork, remove the strands of spaghetti squash from the shell. Place into a large bowl with butter and Alfredo sauce. Sprinkle with Parmesan, garlic powder, parsley and peppercorn

2. Pour into a 4-cup round baking dish and top with shredded cheese. Place dish into the air fryer basket. Adjust the temperature to 320 Degrees F and set the timer for 15 minutes.

3. When finished, cheese will be golden and bubbling. Serve immediately

Nutrition:

Calories: 375; Protein: 13.5g; Fiber: 4.0g; Fat: 24.2g; Carbs: 24.1g

Eggplant Stacks

Preparation Time: 17 minutes

Servings: 4

Ingredients:

- 2 large tomatoes; cut into ¼-inch slices
- ¼ cup fresh basil, sliced
- 4 oz. fresh mozzarella; cut into ½-oz. slices

- 1 medium eggplant; cut into ¼-inch slices
- 2 tbsp. olive oil

Directions:

1. In a 6-inch round baking dish, place four slices of eggplant on the bottom. Place a slice of tomato on top of each eggplant round, then mozzarella, then eggplant. Repeat as necessary.
2. Drizzle with olive oil. Cover dish with foil and place dish into the air fryer basket. Adjust the temperature to 350 Degrees F and set the timer for 12 minutes.
3. When done, eggplant will be tender. Garnish with fresh basil to serve.

Nutrition:

Calories: 195; Protein: 8.5g; Fiber: 5.2g; Fat: 12.7g; Carbs: 12.7g

Mushrooms with Peas

Preparation Time: 30 minutes

Servings: 4

Ingredients:

- 16-oz cremini mushrooms, halved
- 4 garlic cloves, finely chopped
- 1/2 cup soy sauce
- 1/2 cup frozen peas
- 4 tbsp. maple syrup
- 4 tbsp. rice vinegar
- 1/2 tsp. ground ginger
- 2 tsp. Chinese five spice powder

Directions:

1. In a bowl; mix well soy sauce, maple syrup, vinegar, garlic, five spice powder and ground ginger. Set the temperature of air fryer to 350°F. Grease an air fryer pan.

2. Arrange mushroom into the prepared air fryer pan in a single layer. Air fry for about 10 minutes.
3. Remove from air fryer and stir the mushrooms.
4. Add the peas and vinegar mixture and stir to combine. Air fry for about 5 more minutes.
5. Remove from air fryer and transfer the mushroom mixture onto serving plates. Serve hot.

Veggie Stuffed Bell Peppers

Servings: 6

Preparation Time: 20 minutes

Cooking Time: 25 minutes

Ingredients

- 6 large bell peppers
- 1 bread roll, finely chopped
- 1 carrot, peeled and finely chopped
- 1 onion, finely chopped
- 1 potato, peeled and finely chopped

- ½ cup fresh peas, shelled
- 2 garlic cloves, minced
- 2 teaspoons fresh parsley, chopped
- Salt and ground black pepper, as required
- 1/3 cup cheddar cheese, grated

Directions:
1. Remove the tops of each bell pepper and discard the seeds.
2. Finely chop the bell pepper tops.
3. In a bowl, mix well chopped bell pepper tops, loaf, vegetables, garlic, parsley, salt and black pepper.
4. Stuff each bell pepper with the vegetable mixture.
5. Set the temperature of air fryer to 350 degrees F. Grease an air fryer basket.
6. Arrange peppers into the prepared air fryer basket.
7. Air fry for about 20 minutes.
8. Remove the air fryer basket and top each bell

pepper with cheese.

9. Air fry for 5 more minutes.
10. Remove from air fryer and transfer the bell peppers onto a serving platter.
11. Set aside to cool slightly.
12. Serve warm.

Nutrition:

Calories: 123, Carbohydrate: 21.7g, Protein: 4.8g, Fat: 2.7g, Sugar: 8.7g, Sodium: 105mg

Cauliflower Soup

Preparation Time: 5 minutes

Cooking Time: 30 minutes

Servings: 5

Ingredients:

- 4 Cups of vegetable broth (Low sodium)
- 1 Head of cubed and chopped cauliflower
- 3 Cups of chopped potatoes
- 4 Cups of onion
- 2 large carrots
- ½ Cup of celery
- 2 Tbsp of Raw Coconut Amino.
- 1 Tbsp of Coconuts oil.

Directions:

1. Pour the coconuts oil in the Air fryer
2. Add all of your ingredients into the Air fryer you liner you are using.

3. Lock the lid of your Air fryer; seal the vent of the steam.
4. Press the button "Manual" and "Adjust" the time to 9 minutes of cooking time. Once the pressure is reached, then the countdown starts.
5. Add 2Teaspoons of cashew butter
6. Use the blender to mash the soup and add a few cups of kale for nutritional values
7. Garnish your soup; then ladle in serving bowls
8. Serve and enjoy your soup!

Nutrition:

Calories – 134 Protein – 6 g. Fat – 8 g. Carbs – 12 g.

Lemony Lentil Soup

Preparation Time: 10 minutes

Cooking Time: 25 minutes

Servings: 4

Ingredients:

- 1 tablespoon of olive oil
- 1 medium onion, peeled and diced
- 2 carrots, diced
- 5 garlic cloves, minced
- 6 cups of vegetable stock
- 1 1/2 cup of red lentils
- ⅔ cup of whole kernel corn
- 2 teaspoons of ground cumin
- 1 teaspoon of curry powder
- zest and juice of 1 lemon
- sea salt and black pepper to taste

Directions:

1. Choose the saute function on your air fryer and add oil. Add the onions and carrots and saute for 5 minutes. Stir occasionally until the onions are soft and translucent. Add garlic and saute for 1 more minute, until fragrant.
2. Pour in the vegetable stock, lentils, corn, cumin, and curry powder until combined
3. Make sure to lock the lid and set to "sealing."
4. Press and set for manual high pressure, and adjust the timer for 8 minutes. Cook, then carefully turn to venting for quick release. Once vented, remove the lid carefully.
5. Using a blender, puree the soup until it reaches your desired consistency.
6. Return the puree to the air fryer and stir in lemon zest and juice until combined.
7. Season with sea salt and black pepper to taste.
8. Serve warm.

Nutrition:

Calories – 260 Protein – 16 g. Fat – 6 g. Carbs – 40 g.

Kale Cottage Cheese Soup

Preparation Time: 5 minutes

Cooking Time: 5 minutes

Servings: 4

Ingredients:

- 5 cups fresh kale, chopped
- 1 tbsp. olive oil
- 1 cup cottage cheese, cut into small chunks
- 3 cups chicken broth

- ½ tsp. black pepper
- ½ tsp. sea salt

Directions:

1. Add all ingredients except cottage cheese into air fryer and stir well.
2. Secure pot with lid and cook on manual high pressure for 5 minutes.
3. Quick release pressure then open the lid.
4. Add cottage cheese and stir well.
5. Serve hot and enjoy.

Nutrition:

Calories – 152 Protein – 13.9 g. Fat – 5.6 g. Carbs – 11.7 g.

Broccoli Dip

Preparation Time: 25 minutes

Servings: 4

Ingredients:

- 1 ½ cups veggie stock
- 1/3 cup coconut milk
- 3 cups broccoli florets
- 2 garlic cloves; minced
- 1 tbsp. olive oil

- 1 tbsp. balsamic vinegar
- Salt and black pepper to taste.

Directions:

1. In a pan that fits your air fryer, mix all the ingredients, toss.
2. Introduce in the fryer and cook at 390°F for 15 minutes. Divide into bowls and serve

Nutrition:

Calories: 163; Fat: 4g; Fiber: 2g; Carbs: 4g; Protein: 5g

Mozzarella and Tomato Salad

Preparation Time: 17 minutes

Servings: 6

Ingredients:

- 1 lb. tomatoes; sliced
- 1 cup mozzarella; shredded
- 1 tbsp. ginger; grated
- 1 tbsp. balsamic vinegar
- 1 tsp. sweet paprika
- 1 tsp. chili powder
- ½ tsp. coriander, ground

Directions:

1. In a pan that fits your air fryer, mix all the ingredients except the mozzarella, toss, introduce the pan in the air fryer and cook at 360°F for 12 minutes
2. Divide into bowls and serve cold as an appetizer with the mozzarella sprinkled all over.

Nutrition:

Calories: 185; Fat: 8g; Fiber: 2g; Carbs: 4g; Protein: 8g

Sweet Pepper Poppers

Preparation Time: 23 minutes

Servings: 16 halves

Ingredients:

- 8 mini sweet peppers
- 4 slices sugar-free bacon; cooked and crumbled
- ¼ cup shredded pepper jack cheese
- 4 oz. full-fat cream cheese; softened.

Directions:

1. Remove the tops from the peppers and slice each one in half lengthwise. Use a small knife to remove seeds and membranes
2. In a small bowl, mix cream cheese, bacon and pepper jack
3. Place 3 tsp. of the mixture into each sweet pepper and press down smooth. Place into the fryer basket. Adjust the temperature to 400 Degrees F and set the timer for 8 minutes. Serve warm.

Nutrition:

Calories: 176; Protein: 7.4g; Fiber: 0.9g; Fat: 13.4g; Carbs: 3.6g

Crispy Shrimps

Preparation Time: 15 minutes

Cooking Time: 8 minutes

Servings: 2

Ingredients:

- 1 egg
- ¼ pound nacho chips, crushed
- 10 shrimps, peeled and deveined
- 1 tablespoon olive oil
- Salt and black pepper, to taste

Directions:

1. Preheat the Air fryer to 365°F and grease an Air fryer basket.
2. Crack egg in a shallow dish and beat well.
3. Place the nacho chips in another shallow dish.
4. Season the shrimps with salt and black pepper, coat into egg and then roll into nacho chips.
5. Place the coated shrimps into the Air fryer basket and cook for about 8 minutes.
6. Dish out and serve warm.

Nutrition:

Calories: 514, Fat: 25.8g, Carbohydrates: 36.9g, Sugar: 2.3g, Protein: 32.5g, Sodium: 648mg

Croissant Rolls

Preparation Time: 10 minutes

Cooking Time: 6 minutes

Servings: 8

Ingredients:

- 1: 8-ouncescan croissant rolls
- 4 tablespoons butter, melted

- 1 tablespoon olive oil

Directions:

1. Preheat the Air fryer to 320 degree F and grease an Air fryer basket with olive oil.
2. Coat the croissant rolls with butter and arrange into the Air fryer basket.
3. Cook for about 6 minutes, flipping once in between.
4. Dish out in a platter and serve hot.

Nutrition:

Calories: 167, Fat: 12.6g, Carbohydrates: 11.1g, Sugar: 3g, Protein: 2.1g, Sodium: 223mg

Rice Flour Crusted Tofu

Preparation Time: 15 minutes

Cooking Time: 28 minutes

Servings: 3

Ingredients:

- 1: 14-ouncesblock firm tofu, pressed and cubed into ½-inch size
- 2 tablespoons cornstarch

- ¼ cup rice flour
- Salt and ground black pepper, as required
- 2 tablespoons olive oil

Directions:

1. Preheat the Air fryer to 360 degree F and grease an Air fryer basket.
2. Mix together cornstarch, rice flour, salt, and black pepper in a bowl.
3. Coat the tofu with flour mixture evenly and drizzle with olive oil.
4. Arrange the tofu cubes into the Air fryer basket and cook for about 28 minutes.
5. Dish out the tofu in a serving platter and serve warm.

Nutrition:

Calories: 241, Fat: 15g, Carbohydrates: 17.7g, Sugar: 0.8g, Protein: 11.6g, Sodium: 67mg

Strawberry Cobbler Recipe

Preparation Time: 35 Minutes

Servings: 6

Ingredients:

- 3/4 cup sugar
- 6 cups strawberries; halved
- 1/2 cup flour
- 1/8 tsp. baking powder
- 1/2 cup water
- 3 ½ tbsp. olive oil
- 1 tbsp. lemon juice
- A pinch of baking soda
- Cooking spray

Directions:

1. In a bowl; mix strawberries with half of sugar, sprinkle some flour, add lemon juice, whisk and pour into the baking dish that fits your air fryer and greased with cooking spray.

2. In another bowl, mix flour with the rest of the sugar, baking powder and soda and stir well
3. Add the olive oil and mix until the whole thing with your hands
4. Add 1/2 cup water and spread over strawberries
5. Introduce in the fryer at 355°F and bake for 25 minutes. Leave cobbler aside to cool down, slice and serve.

Grape Stew

Preparation Time: 20 minutes

Servings: 4

Ingredients:

- 1 lb. red grapes
- 26 oz. grape juice
- Juice and zest of 1 lemon

Directions:

1. In a pan that fits your air fryer, add all ingredients and toss
2. Place the pan in the fryer and cook at 320°F for 14 minutes. Divide into cups, refrigerate and serve cold

Raspberry Muffins

Preparation Time: 10 minutes

Cooking time: 20 minutes

Servings: 8

Ingredients:

- ¾ cup raspberries
- ¼ cup ghee, melted
- 1 egg
- ½ cup swerve
- ¼ cup coconut flour
- 2 tablespoons almond meal
- 1 teaspoon cinnamon powder
- 3 tablespoons cream cheese
- ½ teaspoon baking soda
- ½ teaspoon baking powder
- Cooking spray

Directions:

1. In a bowl, mix all the Ingredients: except the cooking spray and whisk well.
2. Grease a muffin pan that fits the air fryer with the cooking spray, pour the raspberry mix, put the pan in the machine and cook at 350 degrees F for 20 minutes.
3. Serve the muffins cold.

Nutrition:

Calories 223, fat 7, fiber 2, carbs 4, protein 5

Oreo Cheesecake

Preparation Time: 30 minutes

Servings: 8

Ingredients:

- 1 lb. cream cheese; softened
- 1/2 tsp. vanilla extract
- 4 tbsp. sugar
- 1 cup Oreo cookies; crumbled

- 2 eggs; whisked
- 2 tbsp. butter; melted

Directions:

1. In a bowl, mix the cookies with the butter and then press this mixture onto the bottom of a cake pan lined with parchment paper.
2. Place the pan in your air fryer and cook at 350°F for 4 minutes
3. In a bowl, mix the sugar with the cream cheese, eggs and vanilla; whisk until combined and smooth and spread this over the crust
4. Cook the cheesecake in your air fryer at 310°F for 15 minutes. Place the cheesecake in the fridge for a couple of hours before serving.

Apple Pastry Pouch

Servings: 2

Preparation Time: 15 minutes

Cooking Time: 25 minutes

Ingredients

- 1 tablespoon brown sugar
- 2 tablespoons raisins
- 2 small apples, peeled and cored
- 2 puff pastry sheets
- 2 tablespoons butter, melted

Directions:

1. In a bowl, mix together the sugar and raisins.
2. Fill the core of each apple with raisins mixture.
3. Place one apple in the center of each pastry sheet and fold dough to cover the apple completely.
4. Then, pinch the edges to seal.
5. Coat each apple evenly with butter.
6. Set the temperature of air fryer to 355 degrees

F. Lightly, grease an air fryer basket.

7. Arrange apple pouches into the prepared air fryer basket in a single layer.
8. Air fry for about 25 minutes.
9. Remove from air fryer and transfer the apple pouches onto a platter.
10. Serve warm.

Nutrition:

Calories: 418, Carbohydrate: 55.2g, Protein: 3.1g, Fat: 22.8g, Sugar: 33.2g, Sodium: 157mg

Stuffed Apples

Servings: 4

Preparation Time: 15 minutes

Cooking Time: 13 minutes

Ingredients

For Stuffed Apples:

- 4 small firm apples, cored
- ½ cup golden raisins
- ½ cup blanched almonds
- 2 tablespoons sugar

For Vanilla Sauce:

- ½ cup whipped cream
- 2 tablespoons sugar
- ½ teaspoon vanilla extract

Directions:

1. In a food processor, add raisins, almonds, and sugar and pulse until chopped.
2. Carefully, stuff each apple with raisin mixture.
3. Set the temperature of air fryer to 355 degrees

F. Line a baking dish with a parchment paper.
4. Now, place apples into the prepared baking dish.
5. Arrange the baking dish into an air fryer basket.
6. Air fry for about 10 minutes.
7. Meanwhile, for vanilla sauce: in a pan, add the cream, sugar, and vanilla extract over medium heat and cook for about 2-3 minutes or until sugar is dissolved, stirring continuously.
8. Remove the baking dish from air fryer and transfer the apples onto plates to cool slightly
9. Top with the vanilla sauce and serve.

Nutrition:

Calories: 329, Carbohydrate: 60.2g, Protein: 4g, Fat: 11.1g, Sugar: 46.5g, Sodium: 9mg

Cinnamon Chocolate Churros

Servings: 6

Preparation Time: 10 minutes

Cooking Time: 8 minutes

Ingredients

- ¼ cup butter
- ½ cup warm water
- ½ cup almond flour
- 2 eggs
- 2 ½ teaspoons cinnamon
- ¼ cup semi-sweet chocolate chips
- 2 tablespoons almond milk

Directions

1. Place water and butter in a saucepan then bring to boil.
2. Once it is boiled, add almond flour to the saucepan then stir until becoming a soft dough.
3. Wait until the dough is soft then add eggs to the dough.
4. Using an electric mixer mix until fluffy.

5. Transfer the fluffy dough to a piping bag then set aside.
6. Preheat an Air Fryer to 380°F (193°C).
7. Pipe several pieces of 3-inch-long dough in the Air Fryer then cook for 10 minutes.
8. Remove the churros from the Air Fryer then repeat with the remaining dough.
9. Meanwhile, place semi-sweet chocolate chips in a microwave-safe bowl. Melt the butter in the microwave.
10. Pour almond milk into the melted chocolate then stir until incorporated.
11. Arrange the churros on a serving dish then drizzle melted chocolate over the churros.
12. Sprinkle cinnamon on top then serve.
13. Enjoy.

Nutrition Values:

Net Carbs: 3.4g; Calories: 194; Total Fat: 18.3g; Saturated Fat: 10.2g

Protein: 4.1g; Carbs: 5g

Monkey Bread

Preparation Time: 27 minutes

Servings: 6

Ingredients:

- ½ cup blanched finely ground almond flour.
- 1 oz. full-fat cream cheese; softened.
- 1 large egg.
- ¼ cup heavy whipping cream.

- ½ cup low-carb vanilla protein powder
- ¾ cup granular erythritol, divided
- 8 tbsp. salted butter; melted and divided
- ½ tsp. vanilla extract.
- ½ tsp. baking powder

Directions:

1. Take a large bowl, combine almond flour, protein powder, ½ cup erythritol, baking powder, 5 tbsp. butter, cream cheese and egg. A soft, sticky dough will form.

2. Place the dough in the freezer for 20 minutes. It will be firm enough to roll into balls. Wet your hands with warm water and roll into twelve balls. Place the balls into a 6-inch round baking dish

3. In a medium skillet over medium heat, melt remaining butter with remaining erythritol. Lower the heat and continue stirring until mixture turns golden, then add cream and vanilla. Remove from heat and allow it to thicken for a few minutes while you continue to stir

4. While the mixture cools, place baking dish into the air fryer basket. Adjust the temperature to 320 Degrees F and set the timer for 6 minutes

5. When the timer beeps, flip the monkey bread over onto a plate and slide it back into the baking pan. Cook an additional 4 minutes until all the tops are brown.

6. Pour the caramel sauce over the monkey bread and cook an additional 2 minutes.

7. Let cool completely before serving.

Nutrition:

Calories: 322; Protein: 20.4g; Fiber: 1.7g; Fat: 24.5g; Carbs: 33.7g

Cinnamon Sugar Roasted Chickpeas

Preparation Time: 5 minutes

Cooking Time: 10 minutes

Servings: 2

Ingredients:

- 1 tbsp. sweetener
- 1 tbsp. cinnamon
- 1 C. chickpeas

Directions:

1. Preheat air fryer oven to 390 degrees.
2. Rinse and drain chickpeas.
3. Mix all ingredients together and add to air fryer.
4. Pour into the Oven rack/basket. Place the Rack on the middle-shelf of the Air fryer oven. Set temperature to 390°F, and set time to 10 minutes.

Nutrition:

Calories – 111, Protein – 16 g., Fat – 19 g., Carbs – 18 g.

Notes

www.ingramcontent.com/pod-product-compliance
Lightning Source LLC
Chambersburg PA
CBHW070934080526
44589CB00013B/1511